KU-446-643

Wooden Fishing Boats of Scotland

James A. Pottinger

Glasgow Life Glasgow Libraries	
EL	
C 004777562	
Askews & Holts	27-Feb-2013
623.828209411 ⊔	£14.99

First published 2013

The History Press
The Mill, Brimscombe Port
Stroud, Gloucestershire, GL5 2QG
www.thehistorypress.co.uk

© James A. Pottinger, 2013

The right of James A. Pottinger to be identified as the Author
of this work has been asserted in accordance with the
Copyrights, Designs and Patents Act 1988.

All rights reserved. No part of this book may be reprinted
or reproduced or utilised in any form or by any electronic,
mechanical or other means, now known or hereafter invented,
including photocopying and recording, or in any information
storage or retrieval system, without the permission in writing
from the Publishers.

British Library Cataloguing in Publication Data.
A catalogue record for this book is available from the British Library.

ISBN 978 0 7524 8757 1

Typesetting and origination by The History Press
Printed in Great Britain

CONTENTS

ACKNOWLEDGEMENTS

I have photographed boats and ships of all types in a lifetime of haunting harbours, piers, slipways and anywhere that I was likely to see a boat of any kind, large or small, new or old, building or scrapping. Thus the selection of images was naturally difficult, but was primarily governed by the availability of some record of the boat's history.

Information has been culled from a variety of sources: fishermen, almanacs and published sources by a number of co-operating authors. These include the compilers of the valuable accounts of boats built by the companies Jones, Thomson, and Herd & McKenzie at Buckie, which were published by the Buckie & District Fishing Heritage Centre in the town; also the *Fishing News* weekly and their former annuals compiled by David Linkie; and any sources of photos used. To all of these I am most grateful.

Nevertheless, given the many changes of names and numbers in the life of a boat it is inevitable that some errors may have crept in, but I accept that any such mistakes are my own.

Compilation of this volume owes a lot to the development of computers: as I write I am using one on my right to compile the text, while referring to another on my left showing the photographs. The rapid advance of technology unfortunately means my slide and negative scanner is not compatible with the latest PC operating systems, thus it has been necessary to resort to my older PC, now raised up behind me on a stool!

Illustrations are from my own collection unless otherwise stated. I was conscious of the fact that I have very few from the west coast of Scotland, but Peter Drummond has remedied that deficiency with a number of excellent photographs.

Last, but not least, thanks to my long-suffering wife of fifty-five years, who during compilation of my three Scottish fishing boat publications has put up with books and papers scattered all over the house, and still frequently waits patiently on many draughty corners, or, if lucky, in my car whilst I take 'just one more photo'!

INTRODUCTION

It is generally accepted that the wooden fishing boats built in the period between the end of the Second World War and the 1970s were among the most handsome in the Scottish fleet, but sadly age and the inevitable march of progress has seen many of these graceful craft now phased out and fall victim to the saw and torch. This is a factor which has naturally resulted in many of the boats included being recorded as they are being decommissioned. At the time of construction, many of these were designed for a specific mode of fishing which has now changed, leaving the boats to compete with modern vessels designed to satisfy a new set of parameters. The changes in design, construction and economics from the original conditions leave many of these wooden boats as relics of an earlier era. It is for this reason that I have decided to dedicate this volume to these graceful craft.

Initially most wooden boats were built by builders who relied purely on their own innate skill and tradition to fashion these craft; however, the introduction of statutory regulations pertaining to stability and freeboard, as well as other categories, resulted in the designs being prepared by professional designers and naval architects who co-operated with the builders and owners to implement these requirements.

★ ★ ★

Many of the wooden boats were replaced by steel boats, initially the majority being built by the Campbeltown Shipyard and John Lewis of Aberdeen.

The former, a subsidiary of the parent Lithgow group of shipbuilders, built a whole series of very successful boats in varying sizes, and the Aberdeen builders introduced a number of variants of the equally successful Spinningdale class, which in turn were an obvious development of the so-called Sputnik boats. All of these were instrumental in replacing the ageing and increasingly uneconomic near-water trawlers which operated out of Aberdeen.

Although they represented a different style and appearance from the wooden boats most of these were good looking with shapely hulls. In fact, some of these had finer lines than the wooden boats of the same era, which were beginning to be built with much fuller hulls to take advantage of new rules which encouraged a heavier displacement hull on a limited overall length.

The later steel boats were of an entirely different shape, mirroring the fuller lines of the later wooden boats, and with a few exceptions were either of double or single chine.

The universal adoption of bulbous bows was also applied to quite small craft, down to and below the 10m class.

I have tried to employ as wide a scope as possible to illustrate the many facets of wooden construction, from the preparation of the keel and frames through to the final and inevitable sad resting place. The publisher's inclusion of a selection of colour shots is most welcome, and I have included three such views of my own paintings.

As many readers will know, it is sometimes difficult to keep track of the numerous changes of fishing boat names and registration numbers; given that this volume was compiled early in 2012 it will be unsurprising if some of the data is out of date or erroneous by the time of publication. If so, I ask readers' indulgence and I hope that any enjoyment is not diminished.

1

WOODEN BOATS OF ALL SIZES

Perhaps it is ironic that it is only when we see the wooden boats being broken up, or in early stages of construction, that we can appreciate the scale of the effort required to fashion the fairly large baulks of timber into the final shape and form designed to withstand the stresses of wind, sea and weather; though the final elegant and graceful result remains a true testament to the builder's art. Readers will note a fair number of illustrations which show the boats hauled out on a slipway. These are included to allow for study of the underwater shape, which can only be guessed at from the usual viewpoints, at sea or alongside.

The last boat builders in Scotland constructing big wooden fishing boats were the Macduff Shipbuilders, who took the progression of these vessels to possibly the final stage of development suitable for any viable variant of fishing.

Floreat INS147
My post on a website created some debate as to her origins, but this is possibly the boat of this name built by Walter Reekie at St Monans in 1927 as *Floreat* AH32; later becoming SH15 and INS147.

Casemar LH502

The last wooden boat of its class built by J. & G. Forbes at Sandhaven in 1995, seen here with varnished hull, being towed into Fraserburgh Harbour to be fitted out. She was renamed *Prevail II* PD346 in 2008. She moved to Skye in 2009 and took the name *Asteria* BRD250.

Deejay BF257

Built at Macduff for Fleetwood owners in 1977, she fished as a side trawler and was also rigged for scalloping in the Irish Sea. The three-quarter shelter deck was added later. She was decommissioned in 2002.

Zephyr INS6
Built at Dunbar by William Weatherhead and Blackie in 1969, typical of their shapely designs. This photograph emphasises the graceful tuck of the stern.

In 1984 *Zephyr* INS6 landed 20 tons of herring at Inverness, the last such landing there. She has now been transformed into a motor yacht with a light-blue-painted hull. However, the obligatory large wheelhouse and deckhouse cannot disguise her original graceful lines.

Green Pastures BF4
Built as yard No 131 in 1954 by Herd & McKenzie as *Green Pastures* BF4. She was renamed *Provider* TT18 and later was used on the Clyde and based at Cardwell Bay at Gourock for mooring and angling trips as *Spectrum*. Seen lying ashore at Fairlie a few years ago.

Enterprise LK447
This was the biggest boat by David Howarth at Scalloway, Shetland, launched on 22 March 1947
for a Burra Isle partnership and fitted with a Norwegian 120bhp Wichmann engine and variable
pitch propeller. This was the fastest boat in the Scottish fleet at the time at 10 knots. She fished very
successfully and was later sold to Orkney in 1964. Being fairly fine lined forward, she trimmed well
down by the head with a big catch. After decommissioning she was converted to a yacht.

Attain BF97
This boat was the first transom-sterned boat built by the Macduff Boatbuilding & Engineering Co.
when she was launched as a seine netter in 1971. In 1974 she was renumbered PD332, substantially
modified by addition of a shelter deck and new wheelhouse, and later rigged for pair trawling. She was
decommissioned in 2002.

Vigilant UL55

The *Vigilant* was one of the shapely boats built by Alexander Noble at Girvan in 1968.
Originally having the number SY28 and rigged as a ring-net boat, she was renumbered
in October 1977. She made her last departure rigged as a trawler from Lossiemouth in
February 2011 to be decommissioned and scrapped at Macduff.

Another view of *Vigilant* on the Macduff slip. Whilst waiting to be scrapped, some local
enthusiasts wishing to preserve some of the tradition of fishing at Lossiemouth arranged
to have her wheelhouse lifted off intact for possible preservation.

Daisy PD433
Built by Richard Irvin at Peterhead in 1963 as replacement for *Daisy* 334, which was lost in the North Sea in August 1962; the crew were picked up by a Danish boat after over twenty hours in a life raft. She was sold in 1974 and renamed and numbered *Scottish Maid* BF222. She moved to Orkney in 1979 and took number K553, being lost two years later at Staxigoe.

Lilacina BF395
Built by Forbes at Sandhaven in 1953, sold in the 1970s and renumbered LH205. Since then she has been untraceable.

Embrace BCK21
Built by Macduff Engineering in 1954, she was later skippered by a Norwegian who had escaped to Buckie during the Second World War and settled there, after marrying a local girl. *Embrace* was sold out of fishing in 1976 for conversion to a motor yacht.

Vesper II FR453
The *Vesper II* FR453, seen here at Lossiemouth, was an example of a small zulu-sterned boat which was built at Fraserburgh in 1911. Initially these boats were rigged with sails, but gradually they were fitted with inboard engines. At one time she replaced her full-depth rudder and had an under-slung rudder supporting an extension to the aft end of the keel. After sale she was registered as KY36 in 1972, based at Pittenweem, and then AA36.

Vesper, seen lying at Buckie, shows the extreme rake of the sternpost on a zulu. Much of the former timber has been cut off and it is likely that she had an under-slung rudder during her motor fishing career.

Floreat AH68

Built by Jones at Buckie as yard No 174 in 1980 as *Ardency* INS262, she was unusual in having two Gardner diesels geared to single shaft, later replaced by a single Cat. After moving to Fraserburgh in 1993 and being renamed *Golden Gain* FR 59, her next move was to Arbroath, where she was renamed *Floreat* AH68, replacing the *Sharridale* AH68 which sank in 1997.

Julie Anne BCK 140

Built as yard No 267 by Herd & McKenzie at Buckie in 1977 for Buckie owners, she moved to Fraserburgh and was renamed *Three Sisters* FR 96. Converted to trawling in 2000, she next moved to Mallaig, before being decommissioned and broken up in 2001.

Marguerita INS 136

She ran trials in December 1945 as the 61.5ft motor fishing vessel (MFV) 326, which was built by Brooke Marine at Oulton Broad in East Anglia for the Admiralty. She was sold to private owners on 7 October 1946 at Lowestoft and took the name *Attain* INS 136 in the same year, later being renamed *Marguerita* INS 136 in 1975 and seen here as such at Lossiemouth.

Three Bells PD225
Built as *William Wilson II* in 1956 by Richard Irvin at Peterhead. Fished originally as a liner, she then successively took the names *Vernal* BF71, *Livelihood* PD225 and latterly *Three Bells* PD225.

Procyon INS7
Built in 1956 at Fraserburgh by James Noble, photographed with a new steel wheelhouse and casing at Lossiemouth.

Argo FR255
Built in 1966 as the first transom-sterned boat built by James Noble and designed by a minister who had been a naval architect, she was initially used for trawling then scalloping. She was renamed *Glen Farg* FR225 in 1966 and later renamed *Splendour* PD964, then used mainly for prawn trawling. She was decommissioned in 2002.

Hope PD69
Built as a creeler the 36ft *Hope* was built at Peterhead in the early 1960s by A. & J. Buchan, having been designed by John Buchan, a partner in the builders business, who had been foreman at Herd & McKenzie for seven years. Here she is at Burghead with the inevitably less than handsome GRP wheelhouse.

Morayshire INS212
Built by Herd & McKenzie at Buckie in 1948, *Morayshire* is lying at the former Lossiemouth fish market, with Jones slipway in the background, and is rigged for seine netting. She was sold in 1984 for use as a pleasure boat on the Thames.

Harmony INS257
Launched as yard No 271 in 1978 by Herd & McKenzie as a seiner/trawler, for long periods she
fished on the west coast, around places like St Kilda and south to Skerryvore. She was the last but one
cruiser-sterned boat built by the yard. She moved to County Cork in 1995 where she was often pair
trawled. As D207 she was removed from the Irish registry in 2008 and broken up at Kilkeel.

Clupea
Seen here wrecked at Peterhead, she was completed as the 75ft MFV 1195 in 1945. She was built by
Walter Reekie at St Monans, and was acquired by the Scottish Department of Agriculture & Fisheries
in 1948 as *Clupea* and later became *Clupea II*. She was withdrawn from service and laid up before being
sold to R.P.G. Nunan in 1969 and T. Chalmers in 1973.

Alexanders A177

A regular visitor, as a seine netter, to Aberdeen where she fished for a quarter of a century after being built by J.G. Forbes in 1972. In 1999, after being sold, she was renamed *Primrose* FR223 and was decommissioned in 2003.

Faithlie A100

This 108ft trawler was built by the Montrose Shipyard Ltd in 1956 and generally marked the upper limit of wooden boats. She was repossessed by the White Fish Authority in the early 1960s, sold in 1967 and moved to Fleetwood, where she was managed by Cevic Steam Fishing Co. After a long period of lay-up, she was sold to Irish owners at Cork in 1977, taking the number D606.

Brig O' Nelson BCK134

As the 75ft MFV 1099 she was on trials in August 1944 after completion by Humphrey
& Smith of Grimsby. Intended for service in the East Indies, she capsized on
21 December 1945 and, after being salvaged, was sold in 1947, taking the name *Brig
O' Nelson* BCK134, before being renamed *Fisher Laddie* BCK134 in 1952, then PD315
in 1953 and *Spectrum* FR76 in 1956. She was later seen as a diving boat at Scrabster.
(Courtesy of Aberdeen Local Studies)

Branch FR346

Ran trials in February 1946 after being built by Wilson Noble at Fraserburgh as 75ft MFV
1217 with a 160bhp Lister Blackstone engine. In 1947 she took the name *Mary Watt* LK367,
and *Branch* FR346 and *Tea Rose* FR346 in 1957. A regular visitor to East Anglian fishing from
1947, she landed 140 cran in 1950 and 145 cran in 1961, while 117 cran earned her £1,000 in
1964. In 1965 the *Dayspring* FR120 towed her 90 miles to Great Yarmouth after breakdown;
the engine was sent for repair at Manchester and reinstalled in a fortnight. She took the
Madame Prunier Trophy in 1966 with 128 cran. (Courtesy of Aberdeen Local Studies)

Margaret Rose FR 193
Built by Thomas Summers in 1956, she is seen here during the later days of the herring drift net fishing at Lerwick. Whilst still rigged with gallows for trawling, she later had large winch barrels mounted athwart the ship and geared to the trawl winch to handle the tarry buss rope. A beautiful model of this boat was built by Bill Woods.

Kimberley ME20
This 45ft MFV 790 was built by H.T. Percival at Horning in Norfolk and sold to private owners to take the name *Mizpah V* INS99 in 1946. She was renumbered SY242 in 1949, BF355 in 1952 and *Kimberley* BF355 in 1952. Still named *Kimberley*, she is seen here leaving Pittenweem as ME20.

Opportune PD965
Launched as yard No 150 on 29 January 1986 by George Thomson at Buckie as *Moray Endurance* BCK34, she was handed over on 23 May. She was preceded in 1984 by the transom-sterned *Moray Endeavour* BCK17, built by Thomson for the same owners. Both were painted pale blue. She was sold and renamed *Opportune* PD965 in 1998 before making her last trip to Denmark in 2002 to be scrapped.

Mistletoe BCK260
The seine netter *Fidelis* FR404 was built at Macduff as far back as 1967. She was renamed *Fragrant* FR404 and then *Mistletoe* BCK260 in 1982. In 1995 she was re-registered SO220 on arrival at Castletownbere and finally decommissioned at New Holland in 2006.

Crossby BCK 107

Launched on 11 May 1956, she was handed over on 27 July as *Charles Bojer* FD 94, having been built as yard No 47 by Thomson at Buckie. Renamed *Crossby* BCK 107 in 1973.

Constant Friend INS261

One of the later boats operating out of Lossiemouth, she is shown here leaving that port. She was later at Fleetwood and broken up in January 1996. I have seen photographs of her aground in the dock channel at Fleetwood in 1994, but she was refloated and back at sea a few days later.

Halcyon LK467

Built in 1935 at Macduff in Fraserburgh by James Noble as *Halcyon* WK194. She became LK467 in 1960 and then moved to Skye in 1969. She was owned for periods at Dumfries and Girvan, where in 1979 she stopped fishing. She was intended to be converted into a pleasure boat, but was last seen laid up at Staleyburn near Burntisland in a sorry state.

Surina BCK93

Built in 1970 by Jones at Buckie as *Lothian Rose* LH388, she later became *Surina* BCK93 in 1988, before being decommissioned in 2002. She lay for a long time beside the Model Jetty at Peterhead before being taken away to be broken up.

Astra BCK67

Launched by George Thomson on 25 September 1976 as yard No 140, *Astra* INS193, she was handed over on 24 December as seine netter *Astra* BCK193. She was re-registered BCK67 after being sold, then again as FR143 and converted to twin rig. In 2000 she was bought by Macduff Shipyards and took the number BF542, finally being decommissioned in 2002.

Altair BCK266
Built by the Macduff Boatbuilding & Engineering Co. to a Watson design in 1980.
She was rigged for pair trawling in the early 1990s and, uniquely, this distinctive
turquoise-painted boat remained in the same family for the whole of her career until
decommissioning in the 2002/03 programme.

Garibaldi J. LT358
Built by Walter Reekie at Anstruther in 1928 as *Onaway* KY278, in 1930 she became
LO43 and then had a further change of name and number.

Guiding Star ME34
Built by Thomas Summers at Fraserburgh in 1955 with earlier number PD34, she
has been completely transformed by a forward wheelhouse and deck shelter added.
However, these additions did little to improve her original good looks.

Guiding Star PD34
Guiding Star is seen here at an earlier point in her career, coming into Peterhead riding
on the wash of a bigger boat just ahead.

Ocean Wanderer FR946
Built in 1972 by James Noble at Fraserburgh as the ring netter *Silver Gem* CN297 for
an Avoch skipper, she was a sister to *Silver Bell* INS52. She then went to Campbeltown
before returning north and taking the number BF27, being extensively modernised and
converted to twin rig. Sold in 2001, she was renamed *Ocean Wanderer* FR946 and then
decommissioned in 2002.

Sanboanne BCK89
Built in 1959 as *Surmount* BCK89 by Jones at Buckie as a traditionally rigged seiner with
the classic profile (without a whaleback). She was renamed *Sanboanne* with the same
number in 1974, but whilst based at Fraserburgh she was gutted by fire off Shetland with
such severity that some of the fish were cooked in the hold. She was towed into Lerwick
where she was later stripped down and scuttled off Bressay in 1983.

Hopecrest BCK166
As yard No 138 she was launched by George Thomson on 4 October 1975 and handed over on
4 February the next year. She sailed under the same owner until decommissioning on Tyneside in 1997.

Bonaventure FR300
Built as *Xmas Star* FR87 by Noble at Fraserburgh, later she was BF221. She returned to Fraserburgh in
1978 as FR300 and changed name in 1986 to *Bonaventure*.

Press Forward BF29
She was built at Macduff in 1969 and initially fished for herring and whitefish. A shelter deck was added later and she was converted for twin-rig trawling. Decommissioned in 2002, she was scrapped at Sandhaven. (Courtesy of Peter Drummond)

Primrose BF87
One of James Noble's handsome 52ft boats which was built at Fraserburgh in 1954 as ringer trawler FR291. Later she fished mainly for prawns and scallops on the west coast before being decommissioned in 2002.

Carvida FR 347
A typical Forbes 88ft boat completed in 1978, she was renamed *Ocean Dawn* FR 347 in 1989 when replaced by a Miller steel boat of the same name registered as FR 457. She took the name *Pleiades* PD 170 in the early 1990s, and was finally decommissioned in 2002.

Constellation FR 294
Launched by Forbes at Sandhaven in 1965, it is claimed she is the first transom-sterned fishing boat built in Scotland, with a forward wheelhouse and opening in the transom bulwark for operating the gear. She moved to Ireland in 1984, taking the number CN 293, and worked from Kilkeel before being decommissioned in 2003.

Brighter Hope PD113

Built by James Noble at Fraserburgh in 1967 as the *Marwood* BA339, she moved north and took the number WK333 before being sold to a Peterhead skipper who renamed her *Brighter Hope* PD113. Her travels were not over: she then went to Carradale as *Felicity* CN393 and finally to Ireland with number B911 before decommissioning in 2002.

Replenish FR199

This was the hundredth boat built by Richard Irvin at Peterhead and was a typical boat of theirs in 1975, initially operated as a herring pair trawler and then a seine netter for periods. Sold in 1997 and renamed *Bounteous Sea* FR399, she was decommissioned in 2003.

Silver Wave BF372
Pictured at the East Anglian drift net herring fishing, she was built at Macduff.

Ros Donn PD123
Whilst not built in Scotland, this boat fished there for a period. She was built by the B.I.M. boatyard at Killybegs in County Donegal in 1954 and moved to Shetland initially, being renumbered LK703. She later went to Peterhead, re-registered as PD125, as which she is seen here entering the port. She has now been converted to a pleasure boat and much of her history can be seen on her website.

Britannia BA267
The *Britannia* was built by Forbes at Sandhaven in 1964, and was renamed *Golden Dawn* BA267 in 1994. This boat has often been confused as an Alexander Noble of Girvan build. She was decommissioned in the 1990s.

Lynn Marie BCK86
Built as yard No 248 by Herd & McKenzie at Buckie in 1973. On 9 April 2011 she was
hit by the container feeder ship *Phillip* 6 miles south of the Isle of Man, which did not
stop until 20 miles away from the incident. The damage at the bow necessitated her to be
towed backwards to Port St Mary, helped by three other fishing boats. She was repaired
by Macduff Shipyards.

Rowantree BCK136
Launched on 30 January 1975 as yard No 136 by George Thomson at Buckie, she was
handed over on 28 April of that year. She was renamed *Pentland Swell* WK157 in 1999,
and later based at Portavogie in 1998, before being decommissioned in 2004.

Silver Leaf FR93
She ran trials in October 1945, being built by Charles Pearson at Hull as 45ft Admiralty MFV 990. She was sold and took the name *Fragrance* INS259 in 1949 and FR93 in the same year, but was renamed *Silver Leaf* FR93 in 1971. With the dearth of suitable diesel engines, most when built were fitted with the few available Atlantic diesels or Chrysler petrol engines of 60bhp.

Strathgarry PD91
She was built by Gerrard Bros at Arbroath in 1971 as SY88 to a George Watson design
with a forward engine room, later taking the number PD91 and then CN126 as *Bonnie
Lass* SY126.

Willing Lad FR962
Built at Bangor in 1981 as *Willing Lad* B359, she has also borne the names *B Bounty*
PD181; *Wayfarer* BF25; *Ocean Wanderer II* BF25; *Orient Star* FR962; and *Sunlight Ray*
FR962. She was renamed *Velee* FR962 in 2010. On 6 August 2011 she began to take on
water and eventually sank when in the North Minch; the three crew members were
airlifted to safety by the Stornoway search-and-rescue (SAR) helicopter.

Silver Quest FR11 and *Girl Sharon* BA61.

Acacia II BF390
She was built at Macduff in 1981 as a dual-purpose mid-water/bottom trawler, and was later converted to twin rig. In 2002 she replaced the *Pisces* BCK91, also built at Macduff, and moved to Stornoway and was renamed *Astra* SY153.

Dewy Rose FR144

This 59ft boat was built at Fraserburgh by James Noble in 1973 as a dual-purpose seiner/ trawler. As such she seine netted in the North Sea and mid-water herring pair trawled on the west coast. She was later converted to pair trawling and had a three-quarter-length shelter deck fitted. In 1999 she went to Ireland and took the number B901 until decommissioned in 2003 and broken up at Kilkeel.

Clonmore KY340

She was built in 1973 by James N. Miller at St Monans as *Clonmore* KY340, but was renamed *Guide Us* KY340 and fished for ten years at Eyemouth before moving to Gairloch in 2011.

Windsor FR280
A veteran cruiser-sterned boat still fishing in the 1980s was the *Windsor* built by J. & G.
Forbes as far back as 1934. The seine net winch and coiler is belt-driven from an
extended shaft coupled to the forward end of the engine; the warps are taken off the
coiler and then laid on deck. A common rig until the advent of warp bins, net drums
and warp winches.

Strathpeffer BCK95
Built by Thomas Summers at Fraserburgh in 1959 as a seiner/trawler. By 1989 she was N95, based at
Kilkeel, and was finally decommissioned in 1996.

Constant Faith PD344

A typical Watson-designed boat built as yard No 186 in 1985 by Jones of Buckie as *Trident* LK217. She was sold to Peterhead in 1989 and renamed *Constant Faith* PD344, but unfortunately was lost on 30 June 2001, 53 miles south-east of Sumburgh Head, Shetland.

Tyleana BF223.

Built at Macduff in 1976, she was replaced in 1985 by a new boat of the same name, BF61, which was the last cruiser-sterned boat built at the yard, and was renamed *Achieve* BF223. When this boat was replaced by the new *Achieve* BF223 in 1995 she was sold and renamed *Arcana* BF533. Breaking up by Macduff Shipyards was started at the end of September 2010, about 200 yards from where she was launched by the very same builders.

Achieve BF223
This shows the former *Tyleana* BF223 as *Achieve* BF223 on the Macduff slipway.

Suilven IV BCK366
Launched at Macduff in 1984 as the *Chelaris* BF16. She was sold in the early 1990s to Clogherhead, where she was renamed *Arctic Gull* DA4. Back in the Moray Firth in 1995, she was renamed *Suilven IV* BCK366 and fished for prawns before being decommissioned in 2010 and broken up in Belgium.

Bountiful BF79
Launched in 1986 as Herd & McKenzie yard No 289 *Aquila II* BCK43. She was renamed *Chrisona* BF361 in 1993 and then *Bountiful* BF79; she was decommissioned in 2010 and broken up. The raised deck forward is as such to accommodate the warp reels.

Meldarnic II BCK157
As the *Conquest* BCK157, she was yard No 148 launched by George Thomson at Buckie on 28 September 1984, being the fourth of that name for the same skipper from this yard, all of which had numerals adding up to thirteen! She was renamed *Grateful* BF340 in 1996 and *Lead Us* FR938 in 2000. She made the melancholy journey to Ghent for scrapping in 2010.

Sarepta FR207

She was launched at Sandhaven by J. & G. Forbes in 1976 as a dual-purpose pelagic pair trawler and seiner, and was fitted with refrigerated salt water (RSW) tanks in 1978. One of the biggest wooden boats in Scotland at the time, she was a typical Forbes-built boat of that era, originally with an open fore deck and an 850bhp Cat diesel engine. She was decommissioned in 2002.

Constant Faith FR303

She was built by the Macduff Engineering Co. in 1964 as the *Blue Enterprise* LT488, but came back to Scotland and was renamed *Orion* BF432 then LH332. She was renamed *Constant Faith* FR303 on returning to Fraserburgh, then re-registered BA353 in the early 1990s. Fishing from Peterhead, she was decommissioned in 2002.

Silver Harvest BCK 103
Built by the Macduff Engineering Co. in 1966 as BF378, she moved to the west coast and took number BA130 before returning to Buckie and renumbered BCK 103. She was broken up at Macduff in 1994.

Ocean Reward II BCK 150
Launched at Macduff in 1978 as a seiner/trawler, landing on both the east and west coasts of Scotland. Sold in 1991 she took the number PD50, replacing the new skipper's *Auriga* PD474 which had sunk off the Tyne. She left Scotland for Kilkeel in 1996 and was renamed *Strathmore* B788. She was broken up at Kilkeel in 2003.

Choice BCK200

Built by Forbes at Sandhaven as the 75ft *Dauntless II* LK, she arrived at Burra Isle in March 1961 and was the first in Shetland to have a chilled hold. She was later fitted with a whaleback and shelter deck, and went to Buckie in 1988 to be renamed *Choice* BCK200. After she was sold out of fishing, she underwent a year-long refit at Gloucester to be suitable for corporate team-building courses and on such an event went aground on Blyth Sands in the Thames Estuary on 9 August 2001, but was refloated without damage.

Moray Endeavour BCK17

She was yard No 147. Completed in 1984, she was one of two blue-painted boats built by George Thomson for a fish processing company in Buckie, the other being the cruiser-sterned *Moray Endurance* BCK34. She was renamed *Conquest* BCK265 in 2010, retaining the name of five previous boats owned by the skipper's family, four being built by Thomson.

Honeybourne II BF359
This boat was built by Macduff in 1980 to a design by the Napier Company in collaboration with the owner and builders.

Moray Endurance BCK34
Built as yard No 150 in 1986, she was later sold and renamed *Opportune* PD965 in 1998, but was decommissioned in 2002 and joined the melancholy collection of Scottish boats in Denmark. She was one of the last big cruiser-sterned fishing boats built in Scotland.

Reliance BF80

The 59.4ft overall *Reliance* BF80 was built by the then-styled Macduff Boatbuilding & Engineering Co. in 1988 to replace the *Glen Alvah* BF66, primarily intended for west coast operation. She was of a size that did not require a full skipper's ticket and built to her maker's more or less standard design, apart from having cod end hatches on each side abreast the wheelhouse after section. She was sold to Hartlepool in 2009.

Devotion PD217

Built at Fraserburgh in 1978, the 78ft *Devotion* is seen here prior to the addition of a three-quarter shelter deck which was fitted by the Northern Engineering Co. of Peterhead.

Morning Star BF319
Forbes of Sandhaven built this white-painted boat for seven Shetland partners in 1978 as the *Altaire* LK292, a name that was to be perpetuated by a series of big pursers later. She was later renamed *Morning Star*.

Fruitful Bough PD109
Built at Macduff in 1986 and seen when brand new in May that year. She was replaced in 2004 by a steel boat of the same name and number. The former *Fruitful Bough* was then sold and took the name *Regent Bird III* BCK110, but in 2010 was sold on to Cornish owners and Macduff Shipyards carried out an extensive conversion to suit her for gill netting under her new name, *Govenek of Ladram* PZ51, to operate out into the Western Approaches.

Ocean Rose WY170

Jones of Buckie built this boat at their Lossiemouth yard in 1980 as *Margaret H* INS279 and yard No 176, possibly the last boat built there. She later took the names *Betty James* INS279 and *Ocean Rose*. On 6 March 2004 she was run down by the tanker *Reno* off Whitby, hit on the bow and starboard bow and also aft. She was severely damaged and in danger of sinking, but escorted by the Whitby lifeboat she was able to reach port there. Extensively refurbished at Macduff, she later sailed as *Harvest Reaper II* BF117.

Another view of *Ocean Rose* showing extensive damage.

Sharona II LH250
She was launched by Forbes at Sandhaven in 1989, the last of four boats built for the Moodie family of Longniddry. All four were very similar to the standard 75ft and 23ft beam Napier design, this last example having a full shelter deck.

Here is another view of *Sharona II*, on the launching slip at Sandhaven. The excellence of the hull planking is such that it would be difficult to differentiate from the smooth plating of a steel boat. She was renamed *Aurora II* BF812 and finally decommissioned in 2003/04.

Ariane LK 52

The 67.5ft *Ariane*, seen being launched, was built by J. & G. Forbes at Sandhaven, the first of two similar boats destined for Shetland. The boat was designed for the dual purposes of trawling and seining. Unusually she had a combined winch and coiler fitted forward under the shelter deck, with rope bins instead of warp reels, and bag hatches on both sides. As usual with Forbes, the boat was fully ready to move under power. She moved to Ireland in 1998, took the number S275 and was rigged for gill netting. She was decommissioned at Kilkeel in in 2008.

Ptarmigan BCK 26

Built by Herd & McKenzie in 1985 as a pair seiner. She replaced the skipper's previous *Loraley* BCK 42, built at Macduff in 1971. The three-quarter shelter deck had a raised section over the rope reels on the foredeck. Her vertical wheelhouse windows were a recognisable feature on many Herd & McKenzie boats of this era. Sold to Peterhead in 2000, she took the name *Christina K* PD 306.

Progress BF1
Built at Fraserburgh in 1979 by James Noble for a Whitehills skipper, where this evocative view was taken. She was renamed *Rosebay* PD313 in the mid-1980s but returned to Whitehills under her original name in 1988 on delivery of *Rosebay III* PD65. As BF820 she moved to Tarbert in 2010 and was renamed *Maryeared* TT57.

Crimond BCK118
Built by the Berthon Boat Co. Lymington in 1946 as MFV 1225, one of the numerous 75ft boats, and sold on 12 March 1947. She took the name *Elm* BF181 and then *Crimond* BCK118 in 1959. She was decommissioned at Buckie in 1995.

Fruitful Vine BF240
The last of this class of big boats launched by Forbes at Sandhaven, shown in 2000. She was replaced by a new boat from Macduff and on being sold in 2010, when a new steel boat of this name was delivered from Macduff, she took the name *Shamariah* FR245.

Another view, this on the slip at Fraserburgh, shows the full-bodied shape of the final development of the later Forbes-built boats.

Stroma BA62
Built as yard No 29 in 1958 as the *Silver Chord* BA62 and proudly sporting the
Scottish thistle of her builders, Alexander Noble of Girvan. She was renamed *Stroma*
BA62 in 1976; the gutting shelter was added and a new wheelhouse fitted. She was
decommissioned in 1995. (Courtesy of Peter Drummond)

Spindrift BA220
Another boat from Noble of Girvan, built as yard No 75 in 1974, her graceful sheer now
marred by the inevitable addition of a gutting shelter. Originally she was intended to
be just under 25 tons as measured under Part IV of the 1994 Merchant Shipping Act for
ticket reasons. However, with gaining a ticket the skipper opted for an additional extra
plank to add to the freeboard when building. She was renamed *Sharon Rose* SY190 in
1999 when she moved to Stornoway. (Courtesy of Peter Drummond)

Transcend BF61

Built at Macduff in 1985 as the *Tyleana* BF61, she was renamed *Transcend* BF61 with the commissioning of a new *Tyleana* BF223. She began to take on water on 3 June 2008 when 93 miles north-north-east of Shetland. The water appeared to have entered the engine room through the planking near the fuel tanks at around 2050 hours, but despite the use of two bilge pumps and a portable pump she sank at 2345 hours, the crew being rescued by a nearby Emergency Response and Rescue vessel.

Margarets LH232

At 68.9ft, this was the biggest fishing boat built by Alexander Noble at Girvan when she was completed in 1988 as yard No 86, necessitating the construction of a new slipway to launch her. She was renamed *Bountiful* BF79 in 2010.

Prestige INS305
Launched by Jones at Buckie as yard No 179 in 1981 as a seiner, this boat has moved around the coast a number of times. She was renamed *Glenugie* PD347 in 1989, *Brighter Dawn* LK154 in 1999, *Surina* BCK95 in 2002, *Fortuna* LK29 in 2008 and latterly *Resolution* WY78, when she was converted to a pair trawler.

Pathfinder OB181
Yard No 48 built by Noble in 1964 as *Pathfinder* BA252, renumbered OB181 in 1973. She was fitted with a hydraulic trawl winch and experimented with two pedestal power blocks on the port side to handle a ring net. With her partner the *Ocean Gem* BA265 she fished well enough to finance the 89ft Norwegian-built purser *Pathfinder* BA188 in 1973. (Courtesy of Peter Drummond)

Ocean Gem BA265

Built by Noble at Girvan as yard No 49 in 1964. She is shown here arriving at Ayr in May 1992 with a new wheelhouse and gutting shelter on the port side. (Courtesy of Peter Drummond)

Dawn Maid BA249

Another Noble boat, yard No 62, built in 1969 with number CT99 for Isle of Man owners. She was another boat retrofitted with a new larger wheelhouse and the usual gutting shelter, all of which completely transform the appearance. She was later renamed *Dawn Maid* BA249 in 1992, *Spes Bona IV* BA107 in 1995 and *Dawn Maid* TN102 in 2004. (Courtesy of Peter Drummond)

Hercules II LK438
Yard No 60 built by Noble in 1968 as BA7. Later renamed *Hercules II* UL156 in 1977 and finally *Hercules II* LK438 before being decommissioned in 1995. Seen here arriving at Mallaig with fenders as protection when scalloping. (Courtesy of Peter Drummond)

Northern Venture FR14
At the time when Thomas Summers built her as a long-liner at Fraserburgh in 1955, she was the biggest he had launched. This necessitated a new concrete launching ramp that superseded the drop method previously used. She was later converted for trawling in the mid-1960s.

Achieve FR 100
Built by Irvin at Peterhead in 1972, she was later known as *Complete*. She has now been transformed, as the other photograph of her as *Scotia W* (see p. 103) will show.

Prospector BA25
Built as yard No 73 by Alexander Noble at Girvan in 1973 as a ring netter and seen here ready to launch. Since then she has had a varied career under several names. In 1983 she took the number SH2 after being converted for trawling; she later became TT25 in 1991 and N1 in 2006. She moved to Jersey in 2010 and had port number J189. (Courtesy of John H. Murray, Girvan)

Silver Leaf FR93
This was the smallest class of MFVs built for Admiralty use, and was immediately suitable for seine netting at the end of the Second World War when finances were possibly not readily available to many fishermen to purchase the larger classes of MFVs. There was an anomaly of designation, in that they were classed as 45-footers, whereas in fact they were 49ft 9in overall but 45ft between perpendiculars.

Avoca BCK294
The handsome *Avoca* was built by Herd & McKenzie at Buckie in 1980, exemplifying the classic lines and rig of the traditional fly shooter, set off by the grained wheelhouse. She was decommissioned and broken up at Macduff in 2002.

Budding Rose BF156

Built at Macduff in 1972 as the *Antares* BF110, the seiner/trawler was the last boat built at the yard with their stylish wooden wheelhouse, as well as the last to land at Whitehills. She was renamed *Budding Rose* BF156 in 1982, before being sold to Bridlington in 2010 after a major conversion by her builders to a potter. A pot hauler was fitted on the port side and the existing deck shelter extended forward.

Avrella LK174

Built as yard No 29 by George Thomson at Buckie in 1949 as *Lilt* BCK43, in 1963 she was sold for conversion to a yacht but this was not completed. Taken to Macduff in 1964, she was converted for fishing, was renamed *Avrella* in 1965 and took the number LK174 when she came to Shetland. She is reported as having been converted to a pleasure craft based at Largs in 1986.

Amoria FR 375
Built as the *Westhaven* FR 375 in 1954 at Fraserburgh, she took part in the 1964 drift net herring fishing season off East Anglia. She landed 25 crans of herring on 9 October at Yarmouth, taken 80 miles north of the port, which sold for 260s a cran.

Comrades LK 325
Built as far back as 1958 by John Watt at Banff and well over her half century, she is still fishing with the seine net following the pattern of landing each day, mainly on the west side of Shetland.

Edelweiss FR 104

This boat was built by James Noble at Fraserburgh in 1972 as a single rig trawler. She moved to Stornoway in 1999 and was renamed *Comrade* SY337 and her original 111kW Kelvin engine was replaced by a Cummins KT 19 in 2002. Fish-handling arrangements have been modified and elevated net drums fitted.

Helenus BCK64

Built at Macduff as *Helenus* BCK64, taking the name of a well-known Blue Funnel liner. She came to Shetland and took the number LK641, later renamed *Cornucopia* LK641 and *Sharyn Louise* LK250.

Fertile LK425
Launched by J. & G. Forbes at Sandhaven in 1973 as pelagic and whitefish trawler *Mystic* FR124, when replaced by a bigger boat of the same name, FR266, she was sold and renamed *Adele* BF425. After conversion to twin-rig trawling, she moved to Shetland in 2005 and was renamed *Fertile* LK425. She then went to Ireland in 2010.

Serene PD58
I make no apologies for including this shot in colour instead of the black-and-white photograph which was used in my previous book. On the Peterhead North Breakwater conditions were ideal to take this photograph with just the right amount of chop and bright sun swinging around enough to illuminate the bow and wheelhouse. *Serene* PD58 was built at Fraserburgh in 1974 by James Noble.

Sharons Rose LH317

Launched by Jones at Buckie as yard No 190 in 1988 as the *Telstar* LK378 for a Lerwick skipper. Sold and renamed *Sharons Rose* LH317, she later moved to the west coast in May 2000 and was renamed *Betty James* OB955. Unfortunately, on 10 July that year she ran ashore at 2.30 a.m. on the Isle of Rhum after leaving Mallaig on her way to the fishing grounds and was a total loss. After stranding, her crew boarded a life raft and were rescued by the *Arnisdale*.

Fruitful Bough PD109

This nice shot shows *Fruitful Bough* PD109, built in 1986 by Macduff, and the *Amenna* PD227 (ex-*Rhodella* BCK100) built in 1977 by Jones at Buckie, leaving Peterhead on a bright, sunny day. The *Amenna* took the name in 1983 and later became the *Shalanya* AH45.

Colleague BF103

Built by Tommy Summers in 1958 as the *Convalleria* BF103. She was extensively
modernised in 1967 for purse seining but instead operated as a pair trawler. She went
to Northern Ireland from the mid-1960s to the mid-1970s with the same name
and number, but came back to Scotland and was renamed *Colleague* BF103. She was
decommissioned on 15 December 1994.

Quiet Waters III LK209

Built at Macduff in 1980 as a dual-purpose pelagic/whitefish trawler FR353 fitted with
RSW tanks. They were removed when she went to Portavogie as B221 and she later went
to Shetland in 2007. She was lost when she went ashore on Atla Holm outside Hamnavoe,
Burra, Shetland in May last year and broke up, the crew being lifted off safely by helicopter.

Valiant II FR117
She was built by James Noble at Fraserburgh in 1973, later moving to Mallaig, and renamed *Five Sisters*, *Aurora* and *Primrose* FR233 and CY793. As the Portavogie-owned *Supreme* HL1073, she was fitted with a three-quarter shelter deck and new raised aluminium wheelhouse by Mayrock Fabrications at Anstruther in 2008, completely changing her appearance from that which can be seen here.

Amethyst BF123
Built at Macduff in 1975, later fishing on the west coast where she was re-registered BA123.

Prospector BA25
Leaving for trials, *Prospector* has a number of well-dressed passengers and crew aboard. The rig for ring netting is prominent in the photograph, as is the excellent finish of the hull planking. (Courtesy of John H. Murray, Girvan)

Spindrift BA220
Another view of the *Spindrift* (shown earlier), this time as originally built and returning from trials. (Courtesy of John H. Murray, Girvan)

Dayspring II PD288
Herd & McKenzie's yard No 264 was built in 1978 as the fly shooter seiner *Joysona* BCK148. Four years later and based at Peterhead she was renamed *Dayspring II* PD288 and the gutting shelter was joined to the whaleback. Moving to Howth in 1996, she worked off the south coast of Ireland before being broken up at Kilkeel in 2008, giving a credible thirty-two years' service.

Sunset A430
This 49.2ft boat was built at Arbroath in 1960 by Gerrard Bros and worked the seine net from Aberdeen and Peterhead until she was bought by a Seahouses skipper in 2003 and renamed *Good Fellowship* BK172, operating as a prawn trawler.

Kevella BF364
Completed at Macduff in 1980 for a local skipper, but later renamed *Harvest Moon* FR366. When she moved to Portavogie she was renamed *Quiet Waters* B221.

Concorde BF47
Built by Macduff Shipyards in 2000, for a Whitehills skipper, as one of the last of the big wooden boats built in Scotland. With double oak frames, steel deck beams and bulkheads and of greater beam and depth, she introduces a new class of big wooden boat, of which Macduff are possibly the only builder in the UK capable of building. Sold in 2009, she was renamed *Onward* BF440 and was lost to a fire on 11 April 2012.

Rosemary Ann BA279
This forward wheelhouse boat was built as yard No 51 in 1965 by Noble of Girvan. She was renumbered B279 when moving to Annalong in 1992. Originally fitted with a Kelvin R6, she was re-engined with a 150bhp Gardner engine and then operated as a scalloper/trawler.

Ocean Sovereign BCK15
Built by Jones of Buckie in 1985 as yard No 265 for a Buckie skipper as a seine netter, four years later she was moved to Macduff and converted by Macduff Shipyards for twin-rig trawling with the shelter deck extended to the stern. At the end of 2010 she ceased fishing and had her deck machinery removed at Fraserburgh, before making her last journey in a convoy of five boats to Ghent for scrapping.

Alis Wood LK214
Built by James N. Miller in 1970 as a seiner/trawler, she was later renamed *Flourish* BA815 and fished on the west coast before being sold to Bridlington in 2004 and converted from trawling to potting.

Sincerity AH30

After fishing from the east coast for thirty-five years she moved to Stornoway in 2008. Originally built by Mackay's at Arbroath in 1971 as the seiner *Argus* AH30 for a local skipper, she was renamed in 1990 when bought by another Arbroath skipper, and later converted to twin-rig trawling.

Girl Sharon BA61

Built by the Smith & Hutton yard at Anstruther and originally designed for white fish trawling and creeling on the Clyde, she has travelled far and wide around the UK coast since then. She is seen here leaving Fraserburgh with an extension on the aft end of the wheelhouse.

Harvest Reaper BF214

She was still seine netting in the old way in 1983, with a warp coiler and warps laid down along the deck and a powered roller mounted aft. She looked less dignified lying derelict on the pier at Burghead some years later.

Serene INS67

Launched as *Amaranth* INS267 as yard No 175 by Jones at Buckie in 1980, she was renamed *Serene* INS67 in 1993, then INS1027 in 1999. She was converted from seine net and trawler to twin rig.

Our Pride SH77
This boat, seen when new, was built at Macduff in 1984 as a side trawler for a Scarborough skipper but moved to Hartlepool in 2011. She last operated for a while from Mallaig.

Rhodella BCK100
Rhodella was built as yard No 170 by Jones at Buckie in 1977. She later took the names *Amenna* in 1993, *Shalayna* AH45 in 1997 and *Kiroan* AH45 in 2007. She was broken up at Macduff at the start of 2011.

Seagull BF83
Built at Macduff in 1983, she operated mainly from Kinlochbervie until replaced by *Seagull IV* BF74 for the same owners in 1989. She then moved to the Clyde and was renamed *Brighter Morn* CN151 and was rigged for seining. Six years later she moved to Eyemouth and was renamed *Good Hope* GH116. In 2000 she moved to Buckie, taking the name *Aeolus* BCK143, but a year later she moved to Fraserburgh where she was finally renamed *Auriga* FR217. Nine years later she was scrapped at Ghent.

Asphodel FR197
The biggest of three long-liners by Fraserburgh boatyards, built as the 86ft *Strachans* FR197, completed in 1956 by J.G. Forbes at Sandhaven. The others were the 72ft *Welfare* FR379 by James Noble and the 80ft *Northern Venture* FR14 by Thomas Summers. She continued line fishing until the 1970s when she was converted to seining.

Marigold A52

Built in 1962 by Smith & Hutton at Anstruther, she has formerly borne the names *Sincerity* AH89 and *Marigold* AH39. She at times went scalloping off the Isle of Man, suitably fitted with an array of gantries and derricks.

Winsome LK704

James N. Miller built the *Winsome* in 1966 at St Monans for a Shetland skipper, and she fished from Shetland for over thirty years, rigged for seine netting and scalloping. She went to Islay in 1999 but moved to Carradale in 2010. She then went to Kilkeel in 2012 and was re-registered N611.

Lunaria BCK65
Launched on 2 May 1957 by George Thomson as yard No 53, she was handed over on 3 June for a Findochty skipper. She was renumbered B65 in 1990, decommissioned in 1993 and finally burned on Portavogie beach.

Respect BCK216
Launched by George Thomson at Buckie as yard No 144 on 23 March 1978, she was handed over on 4 October. She was often based at Kinlochbervie and was sold to Macduff owners in 1996 and took number BF396 before being decommissioned in 2002.

Dioscuri BF151

Launched at Macduff in 1972 as the seine netter *Dioscuri* BF151 for a local skipper. She later moved to Kilkeel and was renumbered N379 but returned to Scotland in 1984 and was renamed *Sunbeam* KY379, operating mainly out of Aberdeen. She was sold to Whitehaven fourteen years later, and was decommissioned in 2002.

Xmas Rose A635

Built by Forbes at Sandhaven in 1946, she was one of the first big fishing boats they built after the end of the Second World War. She latterly fished from Aberdeen until the 39-year-old boat was run down by a coaster just off Aberdeen and sank on 12 August 1979. My uncle was at the wheel when she was hit broadside on and the sudden impact and sideways thrust turned the rudder with such force that the steering wheel spun round, bruising his ribs.

Watchful BF107
Built in 1958 by Thomas Summers at Fraserburgh, she was the last herring drifter built by this noted builder. She was bought by two Hepburn brothers in 1990 and renamed *Pleiades* BF155, one of four boats of that name they have owned, named after a steam drifter owned by their great-grandfather.

Amity PD177
Launched in 1971 by Herd & McKenzie at Buckie as the *Seaforth* as yard No 236, one of their shapely and graceful seine netters. Fifteen years later she was renumbered PD177. She went to Castletownbere in Ireland in 1999 and moved to the Aran Islands two years on. She was scrapped in 2008.

Radiant Star PD251

The 81ft *Radiant Star* FR127, another of the Forbes big boats, was built in 1973. In 1978 she moved to Peterhead and was renumbered PD251, and as such she is seen here dressed overall in August 1987, but later she reverted to Fraserburgh registration as *Utility* FR393. Crossing the Irish Sea to Kilkeel in 1996, she took the number B393. She was decommissioned in 2003.

Utilise PD214

Built as a seine netter by Richard Irvin at Peterhead in 1957, she has a coiler and stows the warps along the deck – normal practice before the advent of warp bins and net drums.

Minerva BCK24
Built by Herd & McKenzie at Buckie in 1971, when sold eleven years later she took the number FR147.
Sold again to Lossiemouth, she was renamed *Margaret Anne* INS130 and fished regularly on the west
coast, soon to be renamed *Osprey* in 1997 as a twin-rig trawler with a new Mitsubishi engine. She was
decommissioned in 2003.

Radiant Star LK71
She was built by J. & G. Forbes at Sandhaven in 1956 and stopped fishing in 1997. She was then bought
by an American yachtsman and converted to a motor yacht, and was last seen up for sale at $695,000.

Ocean Hunter BCK66
Built in 1972 by Macduff Boatbuilding & Engineering Co., she moved to Ireland in 1996 where a Kilkeel skipper bought her and renamed her *Immanuel III* N887. On being sold three years later she was renamed again, this time to her original name, *Ocean Hunter* N887. She was another boat decommissioned in 2003.

Regent Bird BCK110
A typical Richard Irvin build, completed in 1961 as *Graceful* PD343 to work great lines around St Kilda and Rockall, and seine net in the North Sea. She was renamed *Regent Bird* in 1974. She was renumbered BCK110 in 1988, and lost at the Bay of Skaill, west of Orkney, in 1999.

Freedom CY 194
She was a handsome boat built by James Noble at Fraserburgh in 1968 as the *Strathyre* FR 4. She lay in a dilapidated condition at Peterhead for a number of years.

Replenish FR 199

Built with an open deck and whaleback as a seiner/trawler by Richard Irvin at Peterhead in 1975, she was initially used for herring pair trawling for a period off the west of Scotland, then seine netting out of Peterhead. After being sold she was renamed *Bounteous Sea* FR 399, replacing a boat of the same number and name built by Forbes in 1969. She was finally decommissioned in 2003.

Illustrious BF 438

Launched on 1 October 1956 and handed over on 10 December 1971, the *Illustrious* was yard No 109 by Jones at Buckie. She was later renamed *Chrisannryl* FR 346 in 1984 and *Golden Ray* FR 346 in 1991, before crossing the Irish Sea in 1994 to Portavogie, retaining her name and number. She was decommissioned in 2003.

Aquila PD220
Built in 1988 by Appledore Shipbuilders as a whitefish seiner/trawler for a Peterhead skipper, she was sold to Castletownbere in 2009 to replace the decommissioned *Carnown Bay* D980.

Enterprise ME155
An early cruiser- or canoe-sterned boat, built by Walter Reekie at St Monans in 1931, that worked creels and lines from Gourdon, where she is seen in this view. Paint pots are at the ready, taking advantage of the ebb.

Beryl BF411
Built at Macduff in 1996, she differed from the more or less standard Macduff design in that she had a forward slope to the lower half of her wheelhouse front and high raking casing along the sides of the wheelhouse, which enclosed the exhausts on the port side, and a matching extension to starboard, both sporting a large M. Her crew were lifted from life rafts by the *Onward* BF440 when she began to take on water in the engine room and sank on 22 May 2011, 25 miles north-north-east of Muckle Flugga.

Radiant Star AH34
Built by Gerrard Bros at Arbroath in 1985 for a local skipper, she was later sold to Macduff and converted by the yard there to a twin-rig trawler about twenty years later, renamed *Headway* PD229. Late in 2008 she was sold and again renamed as *Coronata III* BF356.

Gleaner BF444
Built at Macduff in 1982 as *Beryl* BF411, a three-quarter shelter decker. When she was replaced by a new *Beryl* from the same builders in 1994, she moved to the Clyde and was renamed *Gleaner* CN444, replacing the *Brighter Morn* CN151. She returned to the north-east in 2003 and was converted to a twin-rig trawler; seven years later she made her last trip to Ghent for breaking up.

Solan BCK195
Built by Macduff Boatbuilding & Engineering Co. in 1984 as a seine netter, she had a
raised shelter deck forward to accommodate the large capacity warp reels. Replaced by
a steel boat of the same name from the same yard, she moved to Castletownbere and was
renamed D228 before being decommissioned in 2006 and finally broken up at Kilkeel.

Pilot Us LK271
Built as far back as 1931 by Forbes at Sandhaven, she came to Shetland in 1946 and was
a typical fifie-sterned motor boat, as was traditionally built in that era in north-east
Scotland and Fife. With a two-man crew for most of her career, she fished with lines or
seine net until being decommissioned in 2000. Fortunately not having been broken up,
she is owned by the Shetland Museum and has been preserved.

Headway IV PD229
This much-travelled boat was delivered by Gerrard Bros at Arbroath in 1990, but in 1995 she was renamed *Rebecca* WY477, before going back to the north-east of Scotland and taking the number FR103. The original owner bought her back in 1998 and renamed her *Headway IV* PD229, but she moved again to the north-east of England and was renamed *Katie Louise* WY794, and then *Kristanjo* WY794 in 2002. Now renamed *Temeraire* N850, she is based at Kilkeel.

Frugality BCK52

An example of a motorised fifie, this 56ft boat was built at Buckie in 1930 by George Thomson, and is seen leaving Buckie Harbour in 1978. It was much easier to install engines in the less angled sternpost on fifies than zulus, as a false sternpost could be added to compensate for any aperture cut for the propeller, as seen on *Floreat* INS147. On being sold to Ireland she was renamed *Budding Rose* D419.

Kristanjo WY794
Kristanjo is seen here manoeuvring to berth at the ice factory at Fraserburgh.

Tranquillity BF7
Built as the three-quarter shelter decked single and pair trawler *Tranquillity* BF7 in 1983 at Macduff, she was replaced by a new boat of that name and number in 1988 by the same builders. This was the first boat from Macduff Boatbuilding & Engineering Co. to feature a full-length shelter deck. The first *Tranquillity* was then sold to a Pittenweem skipper and renamed *Ardgour V* KY279. In 1995 she was converted to a twin rig prawn trawler, working as the renamed *Watchful* BF107 until making the final journey to Ghent in 2010.

Moremma BCK 135
Built by Jones at Buckie as yard No 191 in 1988, the 75ft *Moremma* was initially registered as BCK 135 and had a distinctive platform linking the tops of the casings on top of the wheelhouse. She took the Peterhead number PD 135 in 1998.

Regent Bird II BCK254

This 80ft trawler was one of a number built by Jones at Buckie for Grimsby, this one as the *Frances Bojen* BCK254. She was part of a very successful pairing with *Margrethe Bojen* BCK111, until the latter sank with all hands near Ekofisk oil field. She was renamed *Regent Bird II* in 1995, replacing an earlier boat of that name, BCK110, built by Richard Irvin in 1961.

Aquila LK319

Built by Forbes in 1976 as the 86ft *Zephyr* LK319 and designed for trawling, seining and pursing, she was the last wooden purser built for use in the UK. In 1980 she was replaced by the bigger, steel-hulled *Zephyr* (2) LK394 in 1980 and renamed *Aquila* LK319. In 1993 she took the number FR175 when sold to Fraserburgh and was later converted to twin-rig trawling before being decommissioned in 2003/04.

A view of the once busy fishing port of Gourdon. The *Intrepid* ME68 was built as the 45ft MFV 991 at Hull, while the middle of the furthest trio is probably the *Girl Margaret* ME106, built as yard No 10 by Alexander Noble at Girvan in 1950.

Aquila FR175

The powerful bow and fore body is clearly shown in this shot of the *Aquila* on the Fraserburgh shiplift. She has four thicker planks running along full length at the level of the turn of the bilge. Due to her success as a purser Forbes fitted her with 60-ton capacity chilled salt water (CSW) tanks in 1978. She last used her purse seine net in 1985 and two years later was converted into a white fish trawler.

Korona LK 149
Seen having a generator installed, she was initially designed as a white fish/drift net herring boat when built at Macduff in 1968, and later converted to a seiner/trawler. She moved first to Portavogie in 1996 and then to Fleetwood in 1999. She was decommissioned in 2002.

2

WOODEN BOATS
IN VARIOUS GUISES

Fortunately not all fishing boats at the end of their fishing career, or when decommissioned, have followed the melancholy route to the breakers. Instead a few have been lovingly restored or converted for leisure or further commercial use. The obvious initial consideration has been the integrity of the hull, and it is a testament to the skill and workmanship of the carpenters and joiners that in many cases only minimal repair has been necessary.

Inevitably it is the deck and timbers, exposed as they are to wind, sun and general wear and tear, that suffer the most, contrasting with the often almost pristine condition of the bulk of the rest of the hull on many boats considered for restoration or conversion. In fact, many wooden boats have been condemned or broken up not because of any structural defects or general deterioration, but instead due to the often encouraged pernicious diktats of legislation devolved from the remote European Common Fisheries Policy.

Some of these boats have undergone major reconstructions to remove all traces of the various succeeding rigs applied since originally built. The *St Vincent* is a good example of this, taking us back to an earlier era when the development of suitable inboard engines was still under development and the provision of sails was still an accepted option. With the conversion of the former *Maggie Helen* to the auxiliary motor yacht *Loki* and also the *Hirta* (ex-*Surprise*), it seems that zulu-sterned boats have a particular attraction. After some years of neglect the *Loki* is fortunately undergoing a substantial refurbishment at the Shetland Maritime Museum at Lerwick.

Possibly one of the most comprehensive and protracted conversions for future commercial use seen lately has been that of the former *Achieve* FR 100; other conversions have been less ambitious. The following images include a few of these at various stages; while most conversions are finished, in many cases as a labour of love, inevitably a few will prove all too great an undertaking to reach completion. Also included are a number of smaller boats which suffer little by comparison with their bigger sisters in terms of grace and looks.

It is when one notes the diversity of shapes and types that we can get an impression of the many facets of wooden construction. Some were built by well-known major builders, who, often in lean times, turned their hand to the production of smaller boats (often termed 'yoles' in the north-east). But equally important has been the contribution by so-called amateur builders. Whilst builders on the mainland of Scotland universally built these yoles to traditional fifie or zulu lines, those in Shetland, reflecting the island's Norse heritage, remained almost universally true to the curved stem and sternpost double-ended clinker shape of their antecedents.

Inevitably the advent of suitable inboard engines had the most obvious influence on the shape of the smaller boats, which in an earlier era were much finer lined to suit performance under sail. This has resulted in greater volume aft to counter both the weight and the tendency to trim aft due to the thrust of the propeller; the changes have applied equally to later boats built in Shetland on generally traditional lines.

Given that the premier builder of big wooden boats in the UK, Macduff Shipbuilders, have not completed a large wooden fishing boat for some time, it is feared that we are seeing the end of the line for these noble craft.

Jessie West FR257
Among the larger class of boats entering the Scottish fishing fleet were former 75ft MFVs, built during the latter years of the Second World War and just afterwards. An example of this class was the *Jessie West*. She was completed in December 1944 as MFV 1073 by Walter Reekie at St Monans. Sold out of service in April 1948, she took the name *Cairngorm* FR257 and later *Jessie West* FR257 in 1959. She is pictured here at Swanwick on the south coast, near Southampton, after conversion to a motor yacht.

A 48.3ft overall zulu-sterned boat being refurbished at Arbroath in April 2008. She was built as *St Vincent* by Stephen's at Banff in 1910 as a sailing lugger .Fitted with a motor later, she fished until the late 1980s. Between the 1940s and 1955 she was WK117, then until 1975 LK272. She was at Grimsby between 1975 and 1980, then at Lowestoft, before becoming a pleasure craft on the Tyne and at Sunderland from the 1980s to 2007, renamed *Nautilus*. She was sold and brought to Arbroath in 2007 and is now fully restored to her original rig.

Ha' Burn BA79
Built in the late 1940s or early 1950s at either Banff, Macduff or possibly Fraserburgh, as BF326. At one time she had the number INS310, and since then she has had a varied career. She sank at Aberdeen after being holed by lumps of ice coming down the River Dee, but was raised and repaired at Burghead. She was on the Clyde when photographed, in East India Harbour at Greenock as BA79; reportedly she was lifted out of the harbour and broken up at Port Glasgow.

The sad remains of the once graceful fifie *Harvest Reaper*, built in 1931 at Fraserburgh, lying on the pier at Burghead with an incongruous-looking GRP wheelhouse. The addition of a GRP wheelhouse on a wooden boat often gives a discordant note, unless it is designed in harmony with the whole. Perhaps this was to be someone's dream ship, but it is likely now to remain a dream.

Tern A879

A perfect example of the good-looking smaller boats produced by boat builders. As yard No 92, she was launched on 24 July 1961 and handed over by the George Thomson at Buckie five days later as the *Rose* BCK161 for a Findochty owner. She was used for a time at Gourdon as a fish farm boat but later was based at Aberdeen, renamed *Tern* A879 and rigged as a small trawler.

Hirta (ex-Surprise)
A Shetland skipper ordered a 35ft zulu from Stephen's of Banff, but as they had already bought wood for a 60ft boat which had been cancelled by the skipper, it was decided that this timber should instead be used for the *Surprise*, which was completed in 1920. She had a 25bhp Alpha engine originally, but as it was too small it was replaced by a 60bhp Kelvin. After fishing in Shetland as LK477 she was sold to Fife, returning again to Shetland before being converted to a ferry/excursion boat and then a motor yacht.

This shows *Hirta* as she was when running as a ferry between Scalloway and Hamnavoe on the island of Burra. This terminated with the opening of the bridge linking Burra, Trondra and the mainland of Shetland. She also made excursions around Foula. Sadly she now appears to be gradually decaying where she is lying up at Macduff.

Honestas
This boat is lying at Buckie in the initial process of being converted into a motor cruiser. She was built in 1960 by Herd & McKenzie for Granton owners as LH370, but later had the number KY370 in 1967 and INS23 in 1972, being renamed *Ardmore* PD107 in 1985. Recognisable by the extended 'wings' on each side of the wheelhouse, she was decommissioned and converted to a motor yacht.

Honestas LH370

Lying at Scalloway on the west side of Shetland. Unusually she has kept her fishing registration number. She can take up to twelve anglers and is fitted out with accommodation to suit day, overnight and longer stays, and can be hired from Highland Sea Charters based at Cromarty.

This image shows two sections of the keel of the 78ft *Starella* on the slipway at Macduff in July 1970. The tapered keelson is shown clamped to the keel. At the time of construction she was the largest built by the yard.

This shows the extent of the construction of a big fishing boat, much of which will be fashioned by manual labour, to assemble the backbone of the vessel (note the foot adzes). This was taken at the Forbes boatyard at Sandhaven in May 1989.

Star of Bethlehem

I cannot give a definite identification of this boat but it appears to be the *Star of Bethlehem* built by Forbes at Sandhaven which I spotted at Southampton. She has been converted into a yacht.

Scotia W ex-FR 100

The ex-*Achieve*, under her new name *Scotia W*, is designed for private charter, which includes four double-berth cabins in addition to the usual cooking, dining and relaxing facilities, all fitted out to a high standard only yards from where she was built. Stripped to her bare hull, which as a tribute to her original workmanship needed little attention, she was re-caulked to ensure a leak-free hull. Her Cat engine, fitted in 1994, was rebuilt from the crankshaft up.

Lothian Queen LH168
Built by Weatherhead at Cockenzie in 1936, she fished until 1985, in both the North Sea and west coast herring grounds. She was requisitioned for war service in the Second World War. At various times she was *Lothian Queen* B141, *Ocean Queen* KY172, *Ocean Queen* LH415, *Ocean Queen* BMN177 and *Ocean Queen* LO131. She was privately owned from about 1985 and converted for cruising. This photograph was taken at Fairlie a few years ago and, with some hull damage aft, this looks like her final resting place.

Loki
The yacht *Loki* was converted from the zulu *Maggie Helen* LK160 by the local Lerwick schoolteacher Tom Moncrieff, here seen aboard. After being laid up for a number of years, she is now being refurbished at the Shetland Maritime Museum. *Lustre* LK315 is in the background.

This shows *Loki* laid up at Lerwick with an earlier design of coach roof. The raised bulwarks were fitted during conversion. She is another zulu, a type which seemed to have a special attraction for ship lovers who are prepared to devote much time and expense to a restoration.

It is always sad to see the last resting place of any vessel, especially a wooden boat, more so when they have been lovingly maintained and could see many more years of service. Here we see the *Athena* and *Kiroan* in their last berth, being broken up at Macduff. The *Athena* LK237 had been owned and fished by the same owners since she was built by Jones at Buckie as their yard No 161 in 1974. (Courtesy of Ronnie Young)

Celerity
This was the first cruiser-sterned boat built by Herd & McKenzie at Buckie in 1933 as yard No 43
BCK142. When fishing in Shetland she was LK187, and kept her number when based at South Shields.
Her original wheelhouse was replaced by the one shown here. Still easily recognisable, I found her at
Vlaardingen in Holland in 1986, converted to a motor yacht.

Fruition

This conversion was built as far back as 1933 as *Gracie* INS265 by Stephen's at Banff. She operated as a ring netter and later as a seiner. She was bought by a Dutch owner around 1989, who spent the next seventeen years replacing much of the wooden structure and generally converting her to the result seen here at Macduff in 2004. There is an illustrated website dedicated to her restoration, voyages etc.

Herring drift netters at the old fish market at Lerwick in July 1972, *Xmas Morn V* FR31 coming in and the *Silver Wave* BF372 alongside another Fraserburgh-registered boat.

Fruitful Bough LK403
This shows the complexity of the framing and structural members incorporated in the construction of a large wooden boat.

The wreck of the *Fruitful Bough* lay for many years on the east side of Trondra on Clift Sound in Shetland. We can see the openings for the warp rope bins forward and the power take-off from the fore end of the engine to drive the winch. Built in the late 1930s as the *Helen West* BF363 by J. & G. Forbes at Sandhaven, she was later fitted for seine netting.

St Vincent 405CY
The transformation of this zulu is now complete.

A number of wooden fishing boats lying at Buckie. Outside is *Integrity* BCK39, then *Braes O' Strathlene* BCK175 and *Lunaria* BCK65, with the *Reliant* BCK40 lying astern, which dates the photograph to sometime after 1983. It is perhaps the stern of *Suilven* BF90 in the right-hand corner.

Sylvanus
This 45ft boat was built by Walter Duncan (Senior) at Hamnavoe on Burra in Shetland in 1910, on the pattern of the traditional sixern open boats as LK171. She followed the usual pattern of seasonal winter haddock line and summer drift net fishing, sometimes at Stornoway. She was fitted with a winch and warp coiler when converting to seine net, latterly being re-engined with a diesel and a new wheelhouse. After decommissioning, she was used by Shetland County Council as a work boat and was broken up in 1972 at Scalloway.

Scottie's Pride LK68
Built at Burra in Shetland by Scott Christie in a small shed on the face of the hill at Freefield. Her design owes little to the traditional Shetland 'model', albeit with the traditional clinker planking of these, but is a powerful seaworthy shape well suited to a variety of fishing methods. This shows her powering south during an annual eela (angling) fishing competition in 2009.

Glad Tidings V
Almost fully planked at Gerrard Bros boat builders at Arbroath. She was built for the Shiel family at
Seahouses, who have been taking boat trips to the Farne Islands since 1918.

Trust PD323

One of the lovely shaped clinker-built yoles, once numerous around the north-east coast but inevitably now lessening in numbers due to age and the march of GRP craft which require less maintenance. Fortunately maintaining a graceful wooden boat such as this is a chore that to many owners is a real labour of love.

Pansy

Built at Macduff in 1938 as BF494, after her career as a fishing boat she has been bought by two members of the North East Maritime Trust and is undergoing restoration and preservation at South Shields.

MFV 96
One of the 61.5ft Admiralty MFVs which formed a welcome addition to the Scottish fishing fleets
at the end of the Second World War, when many fishing boats that had been requisitioned for service
were lost or in poor state of repair. MFVs had been specifically designed to be suitable for conversion to
fishing boats; at the time the MFVs were designed it was felt by Scottish fishermen that this would be
the optimum size to suit their needs. This example was built by Mashford Bros, Cremyll, and ran trials in
August 1944.

Granny Kempock

A 61.5ft boat which at one time was used by Roy Ritchie on the Clyde at Greenock as a ferry. This shows the considerable rocker on the keel forward, the bullseye being prominent. She was built by Kris Cruisers (1934), Isleworth, as MFV 137 and ran trials in June 1944.

MFV 740

The smallest of the MFVs were the so-called 45ft class, although in fact they were 49.8ft overall. MFV 740 was built by J. Bolson at Poole and ran trials in March 1945, and with the shortage of suitable diesel engines was originally fitted with a Chrysler petrol engine, which was replaced by Foden diesel in 1945. She was the last MFV to serve on the Clyde.

MFV 1037

These were 75.5ft overall and this example was built by J. & G. Forbes at Sandhaven, running trials during March 1944. She had a 160bhp Lister Blackstone diesel engine installed. Apart from by size, these could be recognised by the removable deckhouse extension aft and funnel casing, both of which were removed when fully converted for fishing.

Serene BF453

The diminutive *Serene* is another of the small boats that have an immediate attraction, with their attractive lines and overall shape. She was built at Macduff around 1977 and is reportedly at Ullapool now. There appears to be a fair number of cod in the fish boxes – a comment was made that this is more than the monthly quota of today!

Scotch Queen

Built by Humphrey & Smith at Grimsby as the 75ft MFV 1100, she ran trials in August 1944 with a 152bhp Gardner engine. In 1948 she was sold to a Fraserburgh owner and named *Scotch Queen* FR241. On 2 March 1956 she was registered at Lerwick as LK331 by Shetland owners. She was decommissioned on 9 October 1961 and sold to Mobell Marine Ltd of Horndean in Hampshire as a diving vessel, and it is as such that I saw her at Southampton after a conversion which included a stern gantry and enclosed glazed coach roof over the fish hatch.

Another group of boats at Lerwick in the 1960s, *Venture* LK337, *Jessie Sinclair* LK509 and *Maid of the Mist* LK510. The *Jessie Sinclair* was built by Walter Reekie at Anstruther as the 75ft MFV 1166, running trials in February 1945, and served on the Clyde until brought to Shetland in June 1949. She won the Prunier Trophy for a catch of 272 cran, grossing £665, on 28 October the same year. She was decommissioned in October 1984 and broken up.

Another nostalgic look at a group of herring drift netters at the fish market at Lerwick. Identified are, from left to right, *Replenish* LK97, *Brighter Morn* PD339, *Sunrise* FR359 and *Radiant Star* LK71. These boats were operating at the tail end of the drift net herring fishing, and it has been said that it was only at the demise of this activity that boats were really efficiently fitted out and rigged for this fishery; alas, it was too late.

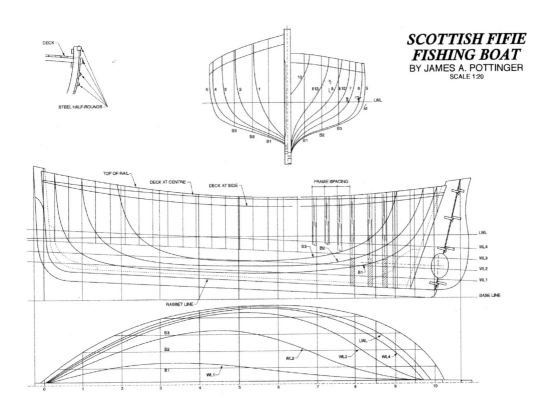

DECK

STEEL HALF-ROUNDS

SCOTTISH FIFIE FISHING BOAT
BY JAMES A. POTTINGER
SCALE 1:20

I drew this model plan of a typical 38ft fifie which is of a type used for line fishing and then seine netting when this was adopted in the late 1940s. The fuller lines aft are in recognition of the need to increase the displacement aft to compensate for the weight of the engine and squat imparted by its thrust. These plans first appeared in *Model Boats* magazine in June 1999.

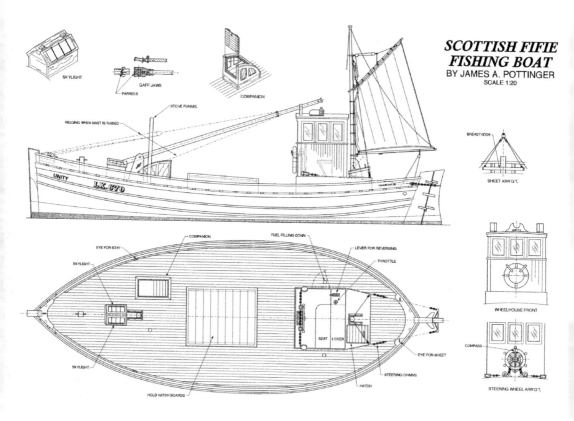

SKYLIGHT

GAFF JAWS

PARRELS

COMPANION

STOVE FUNNEL

RIGGING WHEN MAST IS RAISED

UNITY LK 670

HAMMOCK

SCOTTISH FIFIE FISHING BOAT
BY JAMES A. POTTINGER
SCALE 1:20

BREASTHOOK

SHEET ARR'G'T.

EYE FOR STAY

COMPANION

FUEL FILLING CONN.

LEVER FOR REVERSING

SKYLIGHT

THROTTLE

SEAT L'CKER

EYE FOR SHEET

SKYLIGHT

STEERING CHAINS

HOLD HATCH BOARDS

HATCH

WHEELHOUSE FRONT

COMPASS

STEERING WHEEL ARR'G'T.

A line plan of a fifie, one of about 160 ship and boat model plans I have drawn over the last thirty-five years. I have been gratified to see photographs of numerous models built from these by model makers all over the world.

Yoles

Among small boats berthed at Peterhead, prominent in the foreground are three small fifie yoles, the one on the right having full after quarters, which possibly indicated that she was built as a motor boat. The next, with the finer lines, was most likely originally rigged with a standing lug, the mast being a holdover from then. The GRP boat stern on to the pontoon, second from the left, was the first *Vigilant* PD 542 dory boat when pursing.

Miller boats

Two of the shapely small boats built by Millers at St Monans, used extensively for line and creel fishing (note the powered vertical winch barrel). The full after quarters are typical of this builder's design for powered craft of this size. A later development of this shape can be seen in the numerous cruiser-sterned Fifer motor sailers by the same builder.

The keel, stem and sternpost of a smaller wooden boat, set up in Macduff's wooden boat shed.

Utilise LK3
One of the larger boats built by Duncan Bros, the noted Burra Isle boat builders, in 1962. At 28ft overall, she typifies the modern development of the traditional Shetland sixern of the late nineteenth century. Solely built for use under power, the ends are much fuller with a beamier and deeper hull. She was rigged as shown for mackerel fishing with an array of line reels and strippers.

The steam capstan, used to heave in the net buss rope, which was fitted on the zulu herring drift net fishing boat *Research* LK62. There would have been a small hatch with a roller to guide the rope off the capstan down to the locker below. The capstan main drive engine is on top, with a step up gearing to a small whipping barrel which was mounted on the protruding horizontal shaft. The end of the winch barrel can be seen; this was a later addition on many motor boats in the later days of herring fishing, and was driven by a belt from a drum on the end of a drive shaft taken off the forward end of the engine.

This gives an indication of the massive timbers associated with the big zulu and fifie fishing boats.

If you enjoyed this book, you may also be interested in…

Rough Seas: The Life of a Deep-Sea Trawlerman
JAMES GREENE

978 0 7524 6453 4

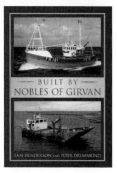

Built by Nobles of Girvan
SAM HENDERSON & PETER DRUMMOND

978 0 7524 5451 1

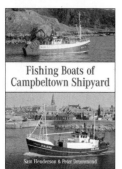

Fishing Boats of Campbeltown Shipyard
SAM HENDERSON & PETER DRUMMOND

978 0 7524 4765 0

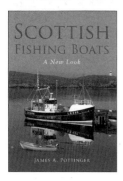

Scottish Fishing Boats: A New Look
JAMES A. POTTINGER

978 0 7524 5304 0

Visit our website and discover thousands of other History Press books.

www.thehistorypress.co.uk